I0607074

Elizabeth Hughes

Woman's manifest destiny and divine mission

In four parts

Elizabeth Hughes

Woman's manifest destiny and divine mission
In four parts

ISBN/EAN: 9783743330849

Manufactured in Europe, USA, Canada, Australia, Japa

Cover: Foto ©Lupo / pixelio.de

Manufactured and distributed by brebook publishing software
(www.brebook.com)

Elizabeth Hughes

Woman's manifest destiny and divine mission

WOMAN'S MANIFEST DESTINY

AND

DIVINE MISSION.

IN FOUR PARTS.

PART I.—WOMAN BEFORE CHRIST.

PART II.—WOMAN AFTER CHRIST.

PART III—WOMAN IN THE TRANSITIONAL PERIOD.

PART IV.—THE NEW DISPENSATION.

BY

ELIZABETH HUGHES.

SAN FRANCISCO:
RICHARDSON BROTHERS, 215 DUPONT STREET.
1884.

WOMAN'S MANIFEST DESTINY

–AND–

DIVINE MISSION.

CHAPTER I.

WOMAN BEFORE CHRIST.

This is so wide a subject, that what I can say upon it will be hardly more than suggestive.

Let us go back to those times of which faint traditions are preserved in so many nations. They are the traditions of the Eden Age, the Golden Age.

Genesis shows us man living on fruits amid the gardenized earth. Woman, free and happy, is by his side. In their perfect love there was no fear. Fear and subjection came afterwards. Eve is nude and smiling, without sin and without shame. Adam, joyous as a child, tends and prunes the trees that are good for food, which in alternate seasons offer a rich repast. Fragrance and bloom encircle their days and nights, there is no chill and no frost. The exquisite harmony of the human frame vibrated in sweet accord to all stellar and terrestrial influences. No disease or discomfort had entered the physical system, the pure blood flushed the cheeks, the rosy limb was perfect in grace and suppleness of motion. The gentle animals responded to man's gentleness; the dark pleading eye of the deer had never been startled by savage pursuit; the birds did not fly away, but welcomed the Eden race with songs and even caresses to their inmost coverts. The souls of this race were as exquisitely attuned to spiritual laws as their bodies were to the sweet harmonies and natural joyous life

of earth. They were obedient children of the Father,—
souls which perchance before their appearance in mortality
had known and kept the Father's laws.

Some of the wise men of the west say that man is the
culmination of and latest development of an ape. There
may be races, or even individuals of all races, of whom this
may be said, or at least suspected. The Eden race does not
answer to this type.

In whatever way plastic matter was molded, it fitted the
needs of pure spirits. The Elohim said: Let us make man
in our own image (plural), male and female created he them.
Eve is said to emerge from her husband's side, symbolic of
their deep interior union,—bone of his bone, flesh of his
flesh,—twain in form as made visible in mortality, but one
in spirit. It was the union of the Infinite with flesh, for a
specific and determined purpose. They were one in divine
essence, even as those who are sanctified are one with our
Lord and Savior, Jesus Christ; heaven was around them,
they came fresh from immortality.

Woman then walked side by side with man, without subjection and without fear. They had simple love and confidence in the powers above, whose they were. There was no
need of rite or ritual. Angelic beings walked and talked
with man,—and there has remained in the hearts of all
peoples a longing for and dim remembrance of that far-off
time.

I find no cause for my infinite desires and prophetic aspirations, within the breast of particled matter. I am belittled
and confounded and indignant, when I hear ape-hood claimed
as my origin. Can the fountain rise higher than the source?
Let those who claim an apish origin content themselves
with their ancestry, and make the best of it. I do not admit
it for myself. As a child of Seth, I am a descendant of the
Eden race, and preserve their traditions. My little fountain
does not rise so high as its source, but it aspires towards it.
I am of noble birth, and of the highest ancestry. I claim
my title, and will wear it, because the cry has been put into
my soul, Abba, Father.

After the terrible destruction of Jerusalem, under Titus, a Jew, named Simeon ben Jochai, compiled a book of the most ancient sacred traditions of his people. It was called the Kabbala, from this is derived our English word Cabalistic, which signifies occult or hidden. He lived a very recluse life, and had many devoted disciples. His sepulchre is in Meiron, in Palestine, even to this day. Not more than two years ago a curious traveler visited it, and found two Jews living in the adjoining chambers. They had lived there for many years, and it was thought that a peculiar sanctity was attached to the place. By means of this compilation many things were preserved that would otherwise have been lost in the dispersion. This work has been greatly prized by many in all ages, and has had thousands of devoted students.

The Kabbala says that the world was formed from the union of the crowned king and queen, emanations from En Soph, "The Boundless One."

Another ancient Jewish book, the Sohar, says: "The agitation and upheaving which is life and motion, is the manifestation of God. Many worlds perished before they came into existence. They were only like sparks, because the sacred aged, or the ancient of days, had not yet assumed his form of opposite sexes, and the master was not at his work; but since then nothing can be annihilated."

It is also stated that souls are pre-existent, and exist in what is called the World of Emanations, before being clothed in flesh. Our Lord, in one place, speaks of the glory which He had with the Father before the worlds were made; and I humbly acknowledge that on this point also I strive to cleave to him, albeit dazzled by excess of light.

It is stated, also, that in this world of emanations, souls are androgenous,—that is, male and female in one,—implying the closeness of the union. They are almost always separated in mortality, and going through the vicissitudes, trials and experiences attendant upon mortal life, are sometimes unmated, sometimes wrongly mated. Our Lord says in the 17th of John, "Thine they were, and Thou gavest them to me, and they have kept Thy word." These souls, however, disjoined on earth, tremble to the infinite source of life, the treasure house of the Father, where they are wrapped in the luminous garment, find all that belongs to them, and rise to the perfection of perfect manhood and womanhood,—neither male nor female,—but a new creature.

The idea of the blending of two souls in one being is illustrated by Balzac, in his strange romance of Seraphita. I prefer, however, to think of them as separate beings with a perfect oneness.

The idea of the restoration of the fitting elements to each other is the dominant note of all romance and poetry. Everywhere, in novels and in song, it is the wail of kindred souls being separated from each other, the incidents of their experiences or the joy of their re-union. The ancient tradition only records a prophecy of the heart, which must somewhere have its fulfilment.

The Kabbala says: Adam and Eve were wrapped in that ethereal substance which is not subject to want, nor to sensual desires. It also says: He (that is man and woman) is the presence of God upon the earth. Transgression has shorn us of our splendor, but infinite love can still radiate through us, if we open our doors to its rays. It makes even our ruins beautiful, and we become the presence of God on earth in a living temple. This radiance is not from us, but through us. This, in its complete state, will ultimate in the restoration of all things, even of our ruins. This will be Paradise regained.

It is very important in these last days to consider the manifestation of the feminine in Deity, and in Humanity, for as a man's God is, or as his idea of God is, so is he, and as a woman's God is so is she.

The feminine is being more and more revealed. Isis is raising her veil. As women, we ought to feel deeply penetrated with the importance, beauty, wonder and mystery of womanhood. I do not believe, as the poor Chinese woman has been taught to believe, that if she is good in the state to which she has been called, she will after a succession of lives in different forms, be changed into a man. I believe and glory in my womanhood, my distinctive, divine womanhood, in which I represent that part of the Elohim in whose likeness I was made. It is true that an eclipse has come, a deep, dark shadow has fallen, and woman has been in the deepest depths of that shadow. She has been a mystery to herself, and to man, often a very troublesome, perplexing mystery, and never more so than now, when she is beginning to recognize in herself powers that not many years ago would have seemed fabulous. We are feeling our way through a labyrinth, in which we can only be guided by a divine thread. Oh, do not let us lose it, for if we do sad disaster may await us.

We will now consider what the tree of life was, and how we lost Eden.

The tree of life in the old Norse traditions was called Ygdrasil; it budded forth in countless generations.

In the Kabbala, the tree of life is pictured in the human form, and the creative organs are pictured as the foundation of life. The full recipiency of life in every portion of the frame into the Eden race sanctified it for celestial uses and inflowed in it the health and happiness of immortality. Man was Wholeness or Holiness, woman was Wholeness or Holiness in every department of being.

The traditions of the Eden race commanded purity. The pure in heart shall see God. It forbade intercourse with another race which already inhabited the earth, with all the stringency with which the Jews were forbidden to associate with the inhabitants of Palestine. When Cain, who was of that wicked one, fled to the land of Nod, he fled to the habitations of a people living on the earth at that time, but totally distinct from the inhabitants of Eden. He belonged to them, he was of them, by the father's side.

The vanity, weakness, and wilfulness of Edenic woman was tempted, and she fell. She in her turn became the tempter, and the ruin was complete. The race which was to be representative of the presence of God on earth failed; they transgressed; the wilful desires of the flesh prevailed against the spirit, and the fruit was death.

From this the sad story of our human experience, the evil and the good, the sweet and the bitter, that fill every mortal life. Ye shall be as gods, knowing good and evil. The access to the tree of life that grew in Paradise was closed; there could be no more access to that tree till Paradise was regained by the work of Christ through sanctification.

What was the first consequence of the Eden failure? The subjection of woman—the natural consequence of such a course. Thy desire shall be to thy husband, and he shall rule over thee—emphasized sometimes by another perversion—thy desire shall be to thy wife, and she shall reign over thee,—both conditions consequent on a fall from the Eden state, with all its love and purity. War and bloodshed followed in the train. Everywhere I saw, as Tennyson says,

> " Beauty and anguish walking hand in hand
> The downward slope to death."

The animal race has never perverted the creative instinct as the human race has. A diabolic force has evidently assailed the fountain of life, the Tree of Life in the midst of the Paradise of God,—witness the monstrous sin of Sodom, the terrible hospitals that show the ravages of deadly, incurable sexual disease; the pitiful form of the leper in his enforced isolation; the poison that in one shape or other taints the life current of humanity, and then ask the mocking tempter where is the fulfilment of his promise—thou shalt not surely die.

Much has been said lately with regard to the laws of heredity, the supreme importance to be attached to good parentage. O, how vital it is! How tenderly to be guarded are the remains of that good, and truth, and purity that the Eden race once enjoyed in their plentitude. Woman was not subject to man then. She was free as the breeze that played around the slopes of Eden.

What is our outlook to-day? We who are descendants of the Eden race in a direct line from Seth. Is it not the old story of the flesh lusting against the spirit? Is not the earth filled with violence as it was in Noah time? And from the same causes: unmitigated selfishness, riotous living and unblessed and discordant unions? Is there any issue for us but in dire defeat and catastrophe with the survival of the fittest, and may it not be time that we thought about building some ark that will ride the incoming angry waves?

Let us look into the times before the flood, when earth was younger and stronger than she is to-day, and nourished a giant brood.

The sons of God saw the daughters of men that they were fair, and took them wives of all whom they chose in the passion of supreme wilfulness. God made and blessed the nuptials of the Eden race, and all the sons of the morning sang for joy; but from these unblessed unions Titans sprung,— mighty men, men of renown, warriors, wonderful inventors. Tubal Cain and his tribe molded brass and iron. They had the strange and wonderful secrets of lost arts. Jubal and his tuneful tribe poured out entrancing music; there was a gay time of feasting and carousing; beautiful women wore their scarlet letter bravely, and gloried in it. "Was there ever such an age as ours," they said, "such inventions, such progress?" But the earth was filled with lust and violence, till the very elemental forces could no longer bear the disorders, for the conditions of man to a greater extent than is generally supposed, affect the planet on which he lives.

So the fountains of the great deep were broken up and Atlantis was overwhelmed, leaving a remembrance only in dim tradition and in the gigantic records of the eternal hills. The destruction of an influential portion of the earth's race was achieved, and from the survival of the children of Seth came our Europe to-day—our dominant, English-speaking race, the children of Japheth—the religious culture of Shem, and the enduring strength of Ham.

Woman, during the time before Christ, was sometimes a drudge, sometimes an article of sale and barter, sometimes a priestess or prophetess, sometimes the syren of an orgie.

An oasis sometimes intervenes where a descent of brighter influences seem to fleck the cloud with splendor,—the honored maids and matrons of Rome's earlier day, when life was so noble, so sweet and simple, the beauty and culture of Greece, the grand spiritualty of the Hebrew race. Always where light begins to break, to some extent, woman stands side by side with man, as she did in Eden.

Slowly along the ages walks the silent foot of woman, with downcast eyes, as if ashamed of herself; only sometimes looking upward with a prophetic gaze of far-off hopes:—burden bearers, carriers of water, palace lilies, drudges of the drudge, slaves of the peasant, and last of all, the women of to-day, refusing to be mothers in a dying-out era, in which little faith is left on the earth.

It may help us to understand the position of woman during this period, to take some individual cases, land-marks of the past, women who have so attracted the thoughts and hopes of the world, that their names are ever more remembered either for good or evil.

The first woman of whom we have any record after the flood was Sarah, the daughter of Zerah, in a direct line from Shem, dwelling with her kindred in Chaldea. Zerah started to go to Canaan at an early date in his history, but did not get more than part of the way. He made a settlement where he found wood, water and pasture, and called the place Haran, after his dead son. From this place Abram and Sarah started on their final journey to Canaan. Much is said of the great and extraordinary beauty of Sarah. This was her inheritance from the Eden race. She was a fair woman, tenderly reared in all the simple luxury of a patriarch's tent, a free child of the plains. When they were about to go down into Egypt, Abram did not say to her, Thou shalt not go forth, and I will set guards about thee, as the Turk to-day does with his women. But he says, "I pray thee say that thou art my sister, that my soul may live because of thee."

Sarah was not hidden, nor was she veiled, and the Egyptians saw her, and she was taken into the king's household. Abram had brought this about by the very means he had taken to prevent it. Twice did this happen, once in Egypt, and once in Gerar, but she was delivered. After the victory of Abram over the five kings a wonderful vision is given to him. In the horror of great darkness, emblematic of Egyptian slavery, he sees the lamp and the furnace, the light of divine strength and truth, pass between the slaughtered sacrifices. And the promises given in the tent at Mamre are reiterated to him,—of the child to be born to Sarah, of the numerous posterity, and the land in everlasting possession. But Sarah is growing old, all natural possibility of motherhood is at end—and there is no child in the tent. Abram, discouraged, pleads with the heavenly powers, who have manifested themselves by visible messengers, and he says, "Lo one born in my house is mine heir, even this Eleazar of Damascus." And Sarah, wholly doubting of her delayed maternity, gives her maid Hagar to Abram. At the prospect of motherhood, exultation fills the heart of the Egyptian, for she, too, knows of the promises; the sickness of hope deferred fills the soul of Sarah, and manifests itself in such bitterness that the Egyptian flees. But the Lord sends her back with kind and beautiful promises. She, too, is to be a mother of nations, but she must return to her mistress, Sarah, and tame her proud heart to fill a subordinate place in the household. And she returns, and Ishmael is born beneath the tents of Abram. The old man loves his son—his only son—and he earnestly prays, and says, Oh, that Ishmael might live before thee. The vision again appears, the promises are again repeated; his name is changed from Abram to Abraham—signifying father of a great multitude; and for the first time a covenant is spoken of, which shall bind him and all his generations to the living God forever. That covenant is the sign of circumcision, and it is declared that who so doth not observe this covenant shall be cut off from his people. This rite represents the cleansing that must be undergone previous to the entrance into the heavenly kingdom, the putting off the old man, the subjection of the flesh to the spirit. This covenant, four thousand years old, is in force to the present day. By it the hills and valleys of Palestine are still pledged to the race of Abraham. If he has kept his covenant, God will keep his. Jerusalem is still the Jewish heart home — from England's great statesman to the smallest trader in any land. The scattered people are known every-where—you cannot mistake them. They are rich, prosper-ous, and waiting still. The vision is for an appointd time,—though it tarry, it will come. In the meantime Babylon is a heap,—and oppressed and denationalized fellaheen are all that remain of the once proud Egyptian race.

After the solemn day of the circumcision, Sodom was de-stroyed, and fifteen years later Isaac is born. For thirteen years has Sarah had to watch the growth of Ishmael, ere her arms are clasped around Isaac, and she nurses him at her bosom; but, oh, the long weary waiting time! I seem to see her with sad brows and half-veiled lids, watching the beauty and strength of Ishmael, and the stately step of Hagar, in whom slavery cannot veil the pride of maternity. She sees her slave's eyes seeking the lithe form of Ishmael in his games of mimic war—Abraham's child, born at her own request. Perhaps she regrets the doubting heart that prompted a wish for the child. I wonder if the deep longing for children on the part of Jewish womanhood is not an inheritance from their beautiful ancestress. But she holds him at last, the promised child, and in her exultation she says: who would have said to Abraham that Sarah should have given children suck. Did she not remember the promise in the tent at Mamre, and her laughing response? Years pass and now she hears " the flow of the wondrous stream that rolls by the border land of souls." Dear eyes watch her as she recedes in space.

I have often wondered at the great space Sarah occupies in Bible History. A whole chapter, the twenty-eighth Genesis, is devoted to the account of her death and burial. She was royally entombed. The very choice of the sepulchres of the people of the land where she sojourned were offered to Abraham to bury his dead, but no other place could be found except the cave near the oaks of Mamre, perchance within view of the very spot where, sitting at the tent-door in the heat of the day, Abraham and Sarah received and hospitably entertained the messenger who brought the promise of the birth of Isaac.

Isaac grows, a child of fruition, a child of peace; as a

young man meditative and quiet. He goes forth into the field to meditate at eventide. The Lord brings him a young and beautiful bride, and he is comforted after his mother Sarah's death; and brings his wife into his mother's tent. Life flowed for Isaac in a smooth, bright current. Isaac and Rebecca.lived in Mamre, that was afterwards called Hebron. They were not wanderers, but possessors and inheritors. The peace of patriarchal times flowed round Rebecca—beloved by Isaac, as Sarah was beloved by Abraham. There seems to have been a great love element in patriarchal natures, which harmonizes and solemnizes their domestic relations. Abraham sought no other ties in Sarah's lifetime. He accepted Hagar at her request. Isaac sought none. Jacob had polygamy thrust upon him by a trick; he did not seek it; then he took the maids at the request of his wives. Abundance, beauty, the rearing and bearing of children belonged to the patriarchal age. The source of the generations of Israel was in the eternal hills, nor could it begin to flow until smitten by the hand of God, and the dry rod of Sarah blossomed with the bud of Isaac.

The horror of a great darkness has fallen on Israel, as foretold to Abraham, four hundred years of Egyptian slavery. The next woman that comes upon the scene is the heroine of a successful revolt, an ambitious, impulsive, and inspired woman; Miriam, the sister of Moses. Tried and disciplined by the hardships of her slave life in Egypt, she has yet some taint of the old slave leaven in her blood—the inability to submit to the easy yoke of the rule of God through the appointed leader. She aspired to rule, and in this way drew upon herself condign punishment. The gleams of Eden, up to this date, linger longest on the head of man, and on the head of that noble leader who was so slow of speech, and yet so mighty in deed and in power—most of all.

We will now follow the course of time from the wilderness to the settled possession of Canaan, until we come to the woman who judged Israel under her palm tree--Deborah, the wife of Lapidoth. Caleb, the scout and spy of Joshua's time, had asked for Hebron, the Mamre of Abraham's time, and it had been given to him. After his death, the people intermarried with the heathen, and served their gods;—thence Israel's defeat and bondage, redeemed at times by different leaders,—till, at last, they fell very low, and the Philistines held them in total subjection, and even disarmed them. The spirit of the Lord comes upon Deborah, and she is told to send for Barak. He comes, and she tells him that he must draw toward Mount Tabor, and engage in an apparently most unequal conflict with the formidable army of Sisera, which was supplied with chariots and munitions of war. Knowing that the Israelites were almost unarmed and, besides, discouraged, he refuses to go unless she will go with him. She consents. Notwithstanding, she says, "What thou undertaketh shall not be for thy glory, for the Lord shall deliver Sisera into the hands of a woman." They met the foe with all their resources at their command, and the word comes to her, "This day hath the Lord delivered Sisera into thine hand,—is not the Lord gone down before thee!"

Together they go down into the battle; together they sing the song of deliverance. "The stars," she says, "fought against the oppressors in their courses. The river Kishon swept them away, that ancient river, the river Kishon." Then raising those wonderful Jewish eyes to heaven, I think I can hear her exclaim, "Oh, my soul! thou hast trodden down strength!" It reminds one of another inspired song of another Jewish woman, Mary of Galillee, who ages after said, "He hath put down the mighty from their seat, and hath exalted the humble and the meek." Fitting song of rejoicing for redeemed woman. Not the exulation of strength and power, as in conquering Roman legions, or Macedonian phalanx, or storm of Sea Kings. All that was the power of force, to exalt the mighty. All this marvelous power. and strength of man's energy puts the mighty in their seat, and keeps them there. But this mystic and mighty power, so closely allied with the divine, exalts the humble and the meek woman, and the toiler, the little children and all who are oppressed, and cry out to God, everywhere.

This woman, mighty only in the strength of the Lord, sees the enemy go down before her. Though there may be confused shouting, and garments rolled in blood, she lifts no hand to destroy, any more than did Joan of Arc, ages after, when she rode her white horse, and bore the consecrated banner into the thickest of the fight. He hath put down the mighty from their seat. Where, but in the line of inspiration and obedience, can we hope for the restitution of woman to her Eden place, by man's side, together conquering all the power of the enemy? Israel had been bewitched by the Baalim and the Venus Ashtoreth of the Zidonians; their manhood was lost. The inhabitants of the villages had ceased, the highways been unoccupied, because, through fear, the travelers had taken by-ways. Now the women were delivered from the noise of archers in the places of drawing water, and the land was at rest. The spirit of revolt against oppression had come to woman with the spirit of prophecy, and it had succeeded. I linger peacefully and restfully in the shade of the palm trees of Deborah. I think that she found home and rest there, after toil and struggle,—and Israel, rescued, blest and at peace, came up to her for judgment.

That mighty vision passes. What do we next see? The beauty of a soft Zidonian valley, Delilah, the Philistine. The soft, frail, laughing thing, takes captive the heart and senses of the chosen captain of Israel, strong Samson. She has him at her beck. He loses even his intelligence and common sense in her caresses. With what a mocking smile she says, " The Philistines be upon thee, Samson." Does she love him? She loves the shining gold pieces much better. She exists in sense, lives all over in her beautiful body. She is of that order of the daughters of men who have always obstructed the path of the sons of light.

He keeps on confiding in her, as if to challenge any hidden tenderness she may have for him. He is betrayed. Then muttering, "Oh, fool!" like Vivien, she leaves the strong man to his fate. This is another type of the way of putting down strength, but it is the Devil's way, not the Lord's way.

After that, no doubt, Delilah was one of the chiefest women in all Philistia. Ashtoreth Venus had triumphed. She might have been at the festival where her blind lover made sport. She was only moved to laughter by that solemn agony, and might have been entombed with him in the temple; nay, perhaps the very sound of her mocking voice might have urged him on to the attempt.

Let me close the record of the daughters of Israel with the tender sweetness of Ruth,—entering, though an alien by birth, into the very house of David, by love and obedience. Love brought her to Bethlehem, and obedience finished the work.

Pass we now to another land bathed by the waters of the Egean Sea. Greece, the land of art and song. Once it was ruled by a man called Pericles, and by his side was a woman named Aspasia. Under their influence Athens rose to its highest splendor. The Greek women of her time and her class ruled the intellect and the senses. Art attained its highest culmination under their influence. To-day every statue or stone unearthed from those ruins is of priceless value. The human form was developed among these people to its utmost beauty and strength. The glorious marbles that they have left us are eternally young. Beauty was their religion, and the senses were deified. But compassion and aspiration seldom looked out of Grecian eyes. When a spiritual man appeared, who had grown beyond their traditions and their superficial culture, and dared to speak as he was inspired, they poisoned him. His name was Socrates. What comes down to us of Aspasia is the glitter and beauty of her person and intellect, and her friendship for the ruler Pericles. She was bright, while she shone with a cold splendor, in the heavens of Greece; but when she disappeared, she left no long line of warmth and radiance after, as did Mary of Galilee.

Let us now pass to the old historic land of Egypt. Its glories are drawing to a close, and a woman rules it. She appears in the declining splendor of Egypt's power, in the full-blown ripeness that precedes decay. Possessing the magical charm of Egypt, unbounded in will and luxury— the serpent of old Nile—she conquered the Roman conqueror, not with munitions of war, but with silken sails, music, perfumes and revels, as she passed down the Cydnus in all her glory. Her name was Cleopatra. The poisonous fascination of that name endures to-day. That gorgeous passion flower still scents the air. The heavy, sleepy perfume of the forbidden tree, overcoming sense and even reason, drawing mankind to death and the grave through avenues hung with blossoms and its fruit, which whoso scents becomes mad. She leaves him at Actium; the infatuated man follows her, and dies by his own hand. She, too, when the desperate game of life is played, and she sees that all is lost, takes the fatal asp from the basket of figs, invites his deadly bite, and drowses off into forgetfulness.

Antony's conqueror,—olive-crowned Cæsar Augustus,—rules the world. He issues his famous decree for the taxing of the world, and from a little town in the conquered province of Judea a carpenter and his wife come up to Bethlehem to be taxed.

In a very short space we have tried to illustrate some of the experiences of woman up to this date. Her weal and her woe, her bane and her blessings, in the generations before Christ. We have traced some of the manipulations of the feminine element from the earliest traditions to the time immediately preceding the advent of our Lord and Savior, Jesus Christ.

We see from these experiences the immense need of all the purity, consecration, courage and devotedness of woman to enable her to find her way back to her first estate,—being made perfect through suffering. We see that power comes whenever woman has walked with God, side by side with man, even in these remote ages. It is but a short space that she has been able to hold her own in the flowing current of events up to this time,—but that even one such manifestation should have occurred is itself a prophecy. We have also seen the conditions under which some such manifestations have been made. We also see that the Eden traditions were respected through the long line of Jewish history, and that consequently the fate and lot of woman was easier, brighter and clearer among them than among any other race.

Motherhood was respected; family ties were strong. They have kept the ancient symbolic covenant.

CHAPTER II.

WOMAN AFTER CHRIST.

In the complete subjection of Israel, almost in the eclipse of faith, a maid appears, like a new, beautiful, bright star rising over the hilltops of the land of Sarah, the land of Deborah. This time the warfare is to be spiritual, not temporal. A thorough reform is to be inaugurated; spiritual wickedness in high places is to be warred against. The citadel of the Prince of the power of the air, garrisoned with all his legions, is to be assailed. A sword must pierce through the soul of this maiden who holds the morning star. The strife for the possession of the earth is about to begin. It was to be a duel in the spirit, only partly visible as to its immense results on earth.

In former days, the angel Gabriel appeared to Daniel in Babylon by the river Ulai. Then there was hope for the Jewish tree, that it should yet sprout again. Now was come utter subjection and ruin; the long dark vista of the denationalization of Israel, not for hundreds, but for thousands of years. The Roman eagles, dreadful, terrible and strong exceedingly, flew over Palestine. Yet never forgetting, the same yesterday, to-day and forever, Gabriel comes to the maid of Nazareth with brighter cheer than he came to the Jewish statesman in Babylon. Daniel trembled and fell on his face, and retained no strength before that bright and awful Presence. He appears before the maid with a salutation,—Hail thou that art highly favored, blessed art thou among women. Mary does not tremble, neither does she fall on her face. With an earnest, enquiring look, she casts about in her mind what manner of salutation this might be. Then was unfolded to her the message of her mysterious conception, and promised maternity. The maid listens with rapt attention, a holy inspiration that casts out fear, for the divine strength and power is within her, and around her.

She simply replies, but oh how grandly, how sublimely,—
" Behold the handmaid of the Lord! be it unto me according
to thy word." Yea, though a sword should pierce her heart,
she accepted it all. The angel spoke of her wonderful child
as one who should reign over the house of Jacob for ever
and ever; and that of his kingdom there should be no end;
an earthly sovereignty; a temporal dominion, sure to be fulfilled, though not yet come; delayed for thousands of years,
while the spiritual fight with the powers in high places which
we understand better than Mary could, is still in victorious
progress. She understood that she was to be the mother of
the temporal Saviour of her people, and the vision is yet for
an appointed time; though it tarry, it will come. Thy cousin
Elizabeth, he said, is about to bear a child, and this is the
sixth month with her who was called barren. The beautiful
and wondrous Presence passes from her; and with great
haste she goes into the hill country of Bethlehem, to the
house of cousin Elizabeth, and salutes her in grave, sweet
Oriental fashion; but Elizabeth exclaims: " As soon as the
voice of thy salutation sounded on mine ears, the babe
leaped in my womb for joy;" and then she reverently and
humbly salutes her as the mother of her Lord, and blessed
is she that believed, for there shall be a performance of the
things which were spoken. Then Mary replies in that wonderful, glorious outburst of inspiration called the Magnificent, everywhere sung and chanted throughout the world to-
day: " My soul doth magnify the Lord and my spirit hath
rejoiced in God my Saviour." Luke i, xlvi, lv. Three
months these loving, inspired women dwelt together, Mary
probably remaining till after the birth of John, when she
returned to her own city, pondering these things in her heart.
Much has been said with regard to the conception of Jesus.
Scientists cannot fully explain the mystery of any mortal
birth; how the wonderful possibilities of a human being
arise from the unknown, and depart unto the unknown. If
we cannot fully unveil the strangeness and mystery of our
own exits and entrances, how can we unveil the laws of the
birth of the bright conqueror of the powers of darkness, our
Lord and Savior Jesus Christ? The joy of Mary in her pros-

pective maternity did not probably go as far as this. She might think perhaps of a little hand that might one day grasp the sword of Gideon, or of Judas Maccabeus, as the disciples did at a later date, when they asked him: "Lord, wilt thou at this time restore again the kingdom to Israel?"

Mary, you did not know that the whole earth was hushed in peace, and waiting for thy divine motherhood, which had been foreshadowed to many nations: that in the forests of Gaul, Druids were raising altars to the Virgin who was to bring forth; that in Syria, Magi were scanning the skies, observing thy star; that even in victorious Rome, the Sybilline books told of the Virgin and Divine child, of the serpent vanquished, and of the restoration of the golden age.

. Whence all this peace and hushed expectation, and the Herald angel's song? Woman had turned her face towards Paradise. Paradise in Hebrew means a place of delights; in Arabic it means a place for the feeding of flocks. How often are we told of the one fold, and one shepherd; "Feed my sheep;" "Other sheep I have which are not of this fold." In these sweet and gentle similitudes are imaged the Paradise of the good shepherd; the green pastures; the still water. "Thou restorest my soul!"

Mary holds her babe in her arms; the diabolic powers incensed because wise men from far Chaldea have recognized him, and brought costly gifts, hailing him as King of the Jews, stir up the jealousy of Herod to destroy him. So Joseph, Mary and the babe flee into Egypt, a journey of about eight hundred miles. They reach Heliopolis, the city of the sun, and take up their abode near the sycamores and sweet waters of Metaireh. They remain there seven years, but on Herod's death return to Judea. About two years after his return from that long Egyptian sojourn came the first recorded gleam of his divine mission at Jerusalem, at the feast of the Passover. The boy, separated from his parents, was talking with the doctors in the temple. It is related that they exclaimed, "this is either Daniel, or an angel;" but Mary coming up, seeking her son, said, "It is Jesus;" and then tenderly and anxiously, "My son, why hast thou done this? thy father and I sought thee, sorrowing."

Then the light shone forth, the light that never was seen before on sea or land, the light of Him who was with His Father before all worlds, and he said, "How is it that ye sought me; wist ye not that I must be about my Father's business?" But he returned with them to Nazareth, and remained subject unto them. For eighteen years, their home life flowed on in that pleasant town, situated on a mountain slope, looking on to a delightful plain. Joseph made ploughs, yokes, and carts, and sometimes built houses. Mary went to the village fountain for water, and washed the clothing in the sweet running streams. Their principal fare probably consisted of loaves of barley and doura, dates, butter, cheese, and dried and fresh fruits and herbs. Sweet soul-fraught years of peaceful preparation. Then the impulse of his mission came upon him, and Jesus and Mary separated. She heard of his baptism, of his fasting in the wilderness. The power of the spirit is upon Him; he is going forth to conquer, but not to conquer the Roman power; a mightier kingdom is to be overcome; the diabolic power which holds the world in possession, with all its legions of disease and death. The captain of our salvation fights palsy, blindness, leprosy, devils, and all manner of disease. He is the Life Bringer, not the Death Bringer, like your Cæsars or Napoleons; yet the world knew him not. His days were filled with incessant work, incessant conflict; devils shrink back; the dead are raised; to the poor the gospel is preached. Everywhere he brought Wholeness, Holiness. Crowds of people gathering in His way, begged of Him life and health. The fierce enmity of the Jewish leaders was aroused. The tender heart of Mary was rent with anxiety for her son. She and His brethren, perhaps near relatives, or even townsfolk, came to Capernaum, where He was, hoping to induce Him to return home with them. While earnestly engaged in His work, some one said, "Thy mother and brethren are without, desiring to speak with Thee," but He replies, "My mother and brethren are they who do the will of God and keep it." But he returned, and the still more ferocious enmity of His own townspeople is roused against Him by His declaration of His divine mission, so that they attempt

His life. We hear afterwards that Mary Mother and the other Marys followed Him, and ministered to Him, even to the foot of the terrible cross. Very early were they at the sepulchre, and tradition relates that Mary Mother first met and spoke with her son, who appeared as a working gardener, while the others were looking into the sepulchre.

Mary Mother continued with the church in Jerusalem for ten years; shared in the wonder and mystery of the forty days after the resurrection, and the joy and blessedness of the Ascension. At the end of ten years, John took her to Ephesus, whither Mary of Magdala followed her. In that beautiful Greek city, Mary of Galilee is said to have dwelt for many years. At last, feeling that the time drew near that she should enter to be where He was, she desired to return to Jerusalem, the beloved but rebellious city, so soon to be destroyed utterly. Not long after she arrived, feeling that her hour was almost come, she desired to see the Apostles and Elders of the Church, and in their presence, and in that of the beloved John, she peacefully departed,—Mary Mother, blessed for ever more. Tradition says that a soft light filled the chamber of death.

Christ never treated woman in any manner that would imply inferiority. His talk with the woman of Samaria was as deep and profound as that with His disciples, if not more so. Deep and profound love, and the joy of service built and cemented the early church with the perfect liberty of love, and the fullness and power of sanctification. Everywhere Christ treated woman without the slightest regard to conventional respectability. She was to Him woman equal and eternal with man, destined in a brighter future to be absolute in harmony and equality, with a divine difference. The subjection of woman had no place under the Restorer of Paradise.

One day He sat at meat in a house of the better class, where, though He and His Disciples had been invited to eat, the customary attention paid to an honored guest had not been shown to Him. A woman enters among the attendants, and gliding to the couch of the Master, for some of the Jews had adopted the Roman habit of reclining at meals, she perfumes his hair with precious ointment. He silently accepted the graceful and customary attention, till roused by the whispered remarks of His Disciples and the disrespectful comments of His host, He quietly and sadly says: "Trouble her not; against the day of my burial hath she done this." It was the consecration of that body so perfect in its glorious manhood, to death, not to pleasure, adding with a profound feeling which showed how deeply the woman's act had touched Him: "Wheresoever this Gospel shall be preached in the whole world, there shall also this that this woman hath done, be told for a memorial of her,"—for the day of his burial!—for few were the days between that social hall and the terrible hall of Pilate. And gliding unchecked to His feet, she anointed them with the same precious ointment and her flowing tears, and wiped them with her long and loosened hair. Profound homage of woman's heart to her best and truest friend. How many women since then have wept at his feet, and He has comforted them, for as He was on earth, so He is in Heaven.

For three hundred years men and women possessed of His Spirit, and, believing in His name, lived as He lived, and died as He died. Long processions of victors, wearing the martyr's crown, stepped inside the heavenly gates. Woman stood side by side with man in the arena, in the flames, in the torture. They were afflicted, tormented, and rejoicing. Marvelous were the gifts and glories of that early day. But the time came when the spirit was lost, and the church leaders sold out to the Emperor. After a while they made the image of the Divine Man a figurehead to back up earthly sovereignty and ecclesiastical tyrannies. The Son of Man, whose life was eminently free, social and humanitarian, was made into a divine idol to countenance the restraints and constraints of the life in death of the convent and cloister. It is true, also, that the iron shell of the convent preserved the thought and literature of former time in the terrible pressure of the crushing out of an old society and the forming a new one. In this mixed condition, scarcely any evil is without its good, nor good without its evil.

The feeling towards woman was such as it had never been before. The worship of Mary gave rise to chivalry, by which woman by degrees became placed in a false position, the recipient of honors she did not always earn or merit; and soon a spirit of sham religion, of scholastic jargon, of melancholy self-introspection, of acrid and wordy disputes, took the place of the grand triumphal faith of the three first centuries. Still, the wonderful ideal of human love blended with divine had come into the world, and some men, touched by the spirit, recognized and felt it. As Dante did in his wonderful love for Beatrice, whom he saw after her death in vision in Paradise among the trees of life. The tenderness of woman was sustained by the divine Ideal, the word manifested in flesh. The wedded pair were emblems of Christ and His loved ones. The seed of the woman bruised the fiery head of the serpent, the deceiving one, by re-baptising and re-creating the whole sexual nature, so that it became re-invested with the divine. The mystery of the new revelation was only the mystery of laws imperfectly understood. There was hope for woman and the toiler. Woman commenced to free herself from the coils of the old serpent of sense and sensuality. A little leaven began to leaven the whole lump. Ascetism and monasticism sprang from the struggles of human souls to meet the serpentine powers and gain the mastery over them; it was a throe of the agony of the new birth. Abelard was the most advanced thinker of his times; the spirit that was within him rebelled at the scholastic learning which had overlaid the grand religious life and faith of the past. He had mastered all its intricacies, and was acknowledged to be the ablest disputant in Paris, a very Paul in the guise of a Doctor of the Sorbonne. He was of a noble family. In those days only two careers were open to the sons of nobles: the army and the church. Abelard chose the latter. He frequented the house of the Canon Fulbert, near the Church of Notre Dame, and there met his neice, Eloise. She was beautiful, aspiring, thoughtful and motherless. Abelard, much older than herself, became her constant companion. They pored over the same books, commented on the same themes, they loved; love explains many mysteries, and the mind of Abelard was never clearer than under the inspiration of Eloise, his devoted pupil. Abelard was a man of noble birth, as well as an abbe, and in accordance with the permissive gallantry of the age, spent much of his time in composing love songs to the young beauty who dwelt in almost conventual seclusion. They were secretly married; love blossomed into fruit. She bore a son, but she refused to permit him to acknowledge the marriage, as she feared it would bar his prospects in the church. She had left her uncle's house, and Fulbert, filled with rage against Abelard, had him seized in the night and mutilated. After the mutilation, Eloise, by Abelard's desire, entered a convent. Abelard gathered some devoted disciples around him, and founded the monastery of the Paraclete, which after a while he gave to Eloise, who retired to it with her nuns and became its abbess. Abelard had a life of toil and struggle. He was too great and too clear-seeing for the age in which he lived. He died at last in a remote monastery in Brittany, and in accordance with his last wishes, his body was brought from Brittany and laid within the chapel of the Paraclete. Eloise and Abelard never met but once after she took the veil, but years after some letters of Abelard's fell into her hands and revived all the old feelings. She wrote to him those wonderful letters, which still exist. She speaks of his name lying so close to the thought of God in her heart, of the recollections of his sojourn in the Paraclete being entwined with every stone. Here she says his eyes had dwelt and his presence filled the day with glory. She tells him that when she took the veil, at his request, it seemed as if the shrines trembled and the lamps grew pale. She says that neither grace nor zeal, but only love was her call, and that she still clings to his love, the divine ideal love which existed wholly apart from the senses, and she begs him to visit her, that his words may direct her to a higher life, which is supreme and eternal. This was a love experience which no woman before Christ could ever have possessed. It was a revelation of the divine matehood.

I can best illustrate the position of woman after Christ by one or two conspicuous examples, landmarks on the sea of centuries—pre-eminently spiritual women, receptive in a great degree of the power which exalteth a people. They all had to stand alone. No Barak was by Joan's side to turn the tide of battle. Eloise was alone in the Paraclete. Years of Madame Guyon's life were spent in solitude and in prison. Woman had to win her way back to Paradise alone, and through suffering. It was for Cleopatra to revel and for Aspasia to triumph; it was for Joan to die and for Eloise to live, which is sometimes the longest martyrdom. Luther's reformation was entirely masculine; it touched only the masculine elements. He was a good husband, and a good father, and a great man, but I do not think ever contemplated the possibility of woman standing side by side with him in any spiritual works. He has impressed that feeling on his followers, whereas the strength of the Catholic Church to-day lies in its recognition of the woman element. The exponent of the reformation in England, Henry VIII, took the abbey lands from the church and gave them to his rapacious followers, under whose exactions England and Ireland are groaning to-day. Luther's reformation was not profoundly social, but the reformation of George Fox, of the Port Royal nuns, and even of Wesley, was. Woman mothered the idea from which sprang social liberty and advancement. It irradiated the world with the Christ spirit. In Pennsylvania, the Quaker, by whose side woman stood with kindly grace, yet with perfect freedom, protected also the Indian and the negro. In the anti-slavery agitation, woman was the friend and co-worker of the noblest, truest men of the age, and oh, if Northern and Southern mothers could have met side by side with our conscript fathers, would that cruel war have mowed down our best and bravest, and would there have been a chance for the dominant party when once fairly seated to grasp the unlimited and almost irresponsible control of the nation's wealth, and by insane luxury pave the way for the downfall of the Republic?

The ideal of Protestantism in Germany and in England is comfort, largely physical comfort, and of woman as a comforter in that sense, which is, no doubt, good as far as it goes. To have a woman who filled all the demands of his life, without infringing on his kingly prerogative, became man's highest aim, and when woman could fill the bill in that respect, it was deemed that she had reached the highest point she ought to hope to attain. Comfort and the idea of woman as supremely connected with comfort, came in with Protestantism, the free towns of Germany and the rise and progress of navigation in England. It was the burgher's ideal. The lady of the middle ages was often the mother of her vassals, sometimes a skilled physician, and even a dauntless warrior. The magic pen of Scott has given life and warmth to these recollections. Fielding and his compeers show the gross sensuousness into which the comfort-seeking type ran, often crowning a series of not very decent adventures with the purely animal-like bliss of mated squirrels.

I will illustrate the possibilities of woman by one of the strangest, most remarkable and saddest lives of the middle ages. There was a time when France was conquered by England, and at her mercy, her King was a fugitive and her people the unwilling vassals of a foreign power. At this time a shepherd girl, with dreamy, meditative eyes, quiet and sedate, is living and laboring at Domreny. Her hard peasant life had strung her nerves and given strength and endurance to her bodily frame. In the field herding her sheep, in the noontide's hush, or in the evening's repose, voices come, and she listens until her love and confidence is won and her heart is inspired. She is loving, obedient and faithful, the Lord's handmaid. This unseen presence fills her soul with peace and rest and gives her power. She was told that she should deliver her country and how she should do it, and the means she should take to accomplish this result. Her hand, accustomed to rude instruments of labor, must bear the sword of St. Catherine. . She should have horse and armor and discern the King in the midst of his nobles. Her mission is coldly and doubtfully recognized, but she goes forth at last, a warrior maid—a consecrated leader. Riding her white horse and bearing her standard, she turns the tide of battle; victory crowns her in many combats. Her King is crowned and anointed in Reims, and the land is freed from the invader. She now asks to return to her father's fields and her peasant life once more. The nobles and generals despised and envied that strange inspired girl, but the people and the soldiers loved and revered her, and the enemy dreaded her, supposing her to be a sorceress. The King entreated her to remain and she consented, much against her will. Alas, for the fatal fight of Compeigne! When leading her soldiers, she was taken prisoner by the fierce Burgundians and sold to the English for sixteen thousand francs. The English warriors dared not, they could not carry out the terrible fate her enemies reserved for her, for this valiant leader was a prisoner of war. So they shifted the responsibility on to the church, and Joan was brought before the ecclesiastical tribunal of the Bishop of Beauvais as a sorceress and heretic, fearful and comprehensive word, often a synonym for all that is noblest. After a period of insulting and torturing imprisonment, she was brought to trial and condemned to be burnt at the stake. Her voices were derided, her mission and herself insulted. The noble soul went up in a fiery chariot. Like her Master, she was martyred by the consent of Herod, Pilate, and the Priests, but she bore witness even in the flames to the truth of her mission. Alone with God she delivered her people. She fought the good fight and received her fiery crown. Countless lives of women have there been, loving as Eloise, glorious as Joan's, devoted as Madame Guyon's. It is the difference in the lift and spring of these lives that should be remarked. The new element that was added, the new victories that were achieved,—and they bore a joyful yoke, an easy yoke, when it became a burdensome, gloomy, sorrowful yoke, it was no longer Christ's yoke, but man's yoke.

We now come to the most striking and important illustra-

tion, the one that most intimately concerns us to-day, because it is a practical illustration of a most vital and
important doctrine—the doctrine of perfect sanctification. It
is the life of Francoise Guyon, a suffering, yet a joyful life;
a bird singing its sweetest songs behind prison bars. She
was beautiful, and of a rich and noble family. In her youth
she loved, but that love was disappointed. "I began," she
says, "to seek in the creature what I had found in God."
According to French customs, a marriage was arranged for
her by her parents, and she was transferred to her husband's
house. But she was no sooner there than she found that it
would be for her a house of mourning. The whole family
was harsh and cold, blind to her merits and rude to her
sympathies. The loving soul, shut out from the natural
possibilities of affection, devoted itself to works of mercy.
She prepared medicines, visited the sick, loaned to me-
chanics, tradesmen and others small sums that enabled
them to start in business, and fulfilled her duties to a sickly
and irritable husband and the children she bore him.

Gradually her spiritual sphere became enlarged. She
held the door open and the divine guest entered. She saw
that the substance of religion is the same in Catholics and
Protestants; that it is always allied to angels and God, and
always meeting with opposition from what is not angelic
and not of God. About this time she experienced sanctification. She says a sanctified heart is always in union with
divine Providence. She became filled with a sense of inward
purity, and from this time was in the enjoyment of liberty.
"Some," she says, "are like a pump, in which the water is
thrown out with effort, but those who are in the enjoyment
of sanctification are like a well." The majority of persons
are brought into this state as she was, through exceeding
afflictions. It was very dangerous at the time in which she
lived, a corrupt time, when insane luxury was preparing the
way for revolution, even to see these things; it was almost fatal
to teach them.

About this time she met with Father La Combe, a soul
like unto hers, purified by affliction and advanced unto consecration and sanctification, a rare soul, but foredoomed to

martyrdom in those days when a corrupt church was nearing its downfall. They had much communion together, sacred hours of interchange, never to be forgotten. She desired that he should become her spiritual director. He at first declined and then accepted that office. More clear-seeing than La Combe and led into a higher experience, she opened to him this hidden way, the divine way of full sanctification. She was shown that this experience strikes at the root of all earthly desire, as well as of all earthly support; that the outward is subject to the inward; that the union with the will of God becomes natural and fixed. Unsanctified passion, she says, loses its power on those who are fully sanctified. The mind assumes a unity of character. The inflowing love of God reduces all principles and motives of action to one. It is revealed to her that she should become the mother of a numerous people, a people simple and childlike (how wonderfully is that fulfilled in these last days!) "My soul," she said, "seemed to pass into God and be lost in Him, as the waters of a river pass into the ocean and are lost in it. This life is an inconceivable innocence."

But Francoise Guyon could not keep the light that was in her from shining out. It shone itself, and she became the inspiration of La Combe, as in later years she became the inspiration of Fenelon. La Combe afterwards began to preach holiness and full sanctification. They had one thought and one object—to lead others into the divine way they had found themselves.

After her husband's death she retired to a convent in Switzerland, and there met with many persecutions. They could not comprehend her nor fellowship with her. A beautiful girl boarding at the convent attracted the attention of a powerful and wealthy priest, but through the influence of Madame Guyon over the girl, his plans came to naught. This added to her difficulties.

She left the convent and went to live in a small cottage with her faithful maid, La Gautiere, and her little daughter. Her household was assailed, her cottage injured, and her garden destroyed. She was very much drawn to the young Swiss working girls. There were some, she says, who worked all day long, and sanctified their work by silent prayer. They would select one of their number to read to them as they worked. After a while she returned to Paris, and while there became much sought after by many distinguished people and ladies of the court. Her influence was widely felt. The sweet, subtle perfume of the spirit was wafted round wherever she appeared. The name of Quietists was attached to those who received these doctrines, and they were declared false, rash and impious, and similar to those of the Puritans of England. Puritanism was agitating England at that time and about to find its outlet in America; but Puritanism was essentially masculine in many of its characteristics. It persecuted Quakers, and hung, on the great oak of Boston Common, Mary Hutchinson, a woman whose soul could not be bound in fetters of their devising, but who preferred freedom and death to the bondage of the spirit. Mme. Guyon says: "He does well who fasts on bread and water, but he does better who fasts from his own desires and his own will. The sanctified soul has power with God and with man."

The sweet, exalted spirit of Archbishop Fenelon recognized her influence. His friendship and profound tenderness and respect for her never ceased till the end of his pure and holy life, but it involved him in a controversy with the narrow soul of Bossuet, and finally drove him into exile, where he quietly and blessedly fulfilled the duties of his episcopate—a true shepherd of the sheep. It was no privation to him to leave Paris; the country delighted him. "In the midst of my duties," he said, "I find God's holy peace." Madame Guyon says: "I presented Fenelon before God in special prayer."

The Port Royal nuns were touched by the divine flame, and brooded under the wings of the Holy Ghost. To them this also brought spoliation and destruction. An armed band despoiled the convent and dispersed the Sisters. An aged nun, the last to leave the ruined building, raising her hand in the presence of the leader of the band and his soldiers, said: "To-day, sirs, is the hour of man, but be assured that another day—the day of God's righteous retribution—

will soon come!" And it came, with the tocsin of revolution, the barricades of Paris, the reign of terror, and the summons of kings and nobles to judgment.

But Madame Guyon's teachings could not go on; these dangerous voices must be silenced. La Combe wrote to her: "The times look heavy; the storm gathers in the sky. I feel resigned to reproaches and ignominies, I am about to suffer. It is my wish that you should sacrifice me to God, as I have sacrificed myself." His presentiments were fulfilled. He was imprisoned shortly afterwards; a life-long imprisonment of twenty-seven years, from which he emerged only to be taken to the hospital at Charenton, where he died. Madame Guyon did all she could for him; sent him money and books, and wrote him comforting and affectionate letters as long as she was able. He wrote her: "All my desires are summed up in one—that God may be glorified in me."

Three months after La Combe's imprisonment Mme. Guyon was imprisoned. She says in her diary: "O Holy Spirit of Love, let me be subject to thy will!" and then, August 20, 1688: "I am now forty years of age, in prison, a place I love and cherish, as I find it sanctified by the Lord."

After eight months she was liberated, then imprisoned again, and at last consigned to the Bastille—that gloomy and terrible fortress of old Paris. This time the imprisonment was designed to crush her, and it did, physically. Her faithful maid, La Gautiere, who had shared her other prisons, was not permitted to be with her. La Gautiere was more than a servant; she was a sister beloved in the Lord. Together had they sung and prayed and given thanks. Some of the sweetest songs of that dear, inspired poet of the New Dispensation came from behind her prison bars. Mme. Guyon looked up in her gloomy cell in the Bastille and saw no sun; that dove of tenderness, who would fain have gone forth, bearing a message of love to every human soul; she, who had lived softly in her sunny gardens, could see no green fields or woods—only iron-bound windows, in the immense thickness of the walls—and more than this, they made her suffer the keenest mental and spiritual torture with diabolic ingenuity.

La Gautiere died in prison. She wrote before her death, "I am in this prison, and Mme. Guyon is in another cell, but we are united in spirit. The walls of a prison cannot hinder the union of souls."

After years of imprisonment, her sentence was commuted into exile. She emerged from this den of torture, sick, and ever after incapable of any active work; a dove with broken wings. But she says, with all her old sweetness, "My life is consecrated to God, to suffer for Him, as well as to enjoy him." And then looking back to the years of her active life, she says: "My mission has been, and is, to lead those who are already beginners to perfect conversion." She was a sweet songstress, a sweet lyrical poet. She left behind her many published works.

It is a relief to think that she saw green fields and the sun once more. The time of her departure came in the beautiful month of June, 1717. She went home in peace.

Such was woman after Christ—one in his love and in the fellowship of his sufferings.

The undaunted heart which beat under Joan's armor was no stronger and no steadier than the loving resignation of Mme. Guyon in the Bastile, or of Eloise in the Paraclete.

CHAPTER III.

WOMAN IN THE TRANSITIONAL PERIOD.

The Transitional Period now opens,—violent and stormy, with the terrible retributions of French revolutions and Napoleonic wars; also, the development in the western world of the great and powerful English-speaking nations of America, and many other signs and tokens. In this period we live to-day, and as time wears on, confusion becomes worse confounded and the babble of voices increases, so that those who in any department give out a clear, audible voice, give out a distinct answer to any question, whether as touching labor, finance, sociology, temperance, or any other vital question ought to be carefully regarded, and what they have to say wisely considered. In England it is becoming a very important question how large masses of human beings are to be housed. Even here it is becoming a question how large masses of people are to be fed, in spite of the immensely increasing average wealth of the nation, but it all goes into a few hands, and the tendency that way is increasing. The English are rebelling against their hereditary house of law makers, of which the late immense meeting of a hundred thousand people in Hyde Park, singing the Marseillaise and crying, "Down with the Peers," is a very significant token.

The frugal, patient Germans are asking why they should feed, pay and clothe thousands of their best producers, who are kept in uniformed idleness and used as a force to tighten the bonds on the people who are supporting them.

Conditions of inharmony in families are becoming more and more trying, two-thirds, or even more of households are places of purgatory, where suffering souls antagonize. The air is charged with unspent forces, "ancestral voices prophesying war." Oh, how precious is every soul that knows how to make its own harmony, and radiates an atmosphere of peace.

Law is no longer respectable; justice is too often a thing
of barter and sale; the church is fast losing its power,
unless as some heaven-endowed men and women make a
spot of radiance and a home of sympathy. Then people
come round to warm themselves by the fire of the spirit,
and are blessed. One feature of our modern society is the
unveiling of shams, and as they are unveiled, it is seen how
defective the underpining of present society is.

We are living under the shadow of the impending wall
which in the interior of the pyramid, is represented
as closing the great gallery of the Christian dispensation.
Woman is awakened by the tocsins of approaching conflict,
which are sounding everywhere. She perceives that she
must eat her bread by the sweat of her brow, and that the
conditions under which she can do so are becoming day by
day more onerous. She is invading, where she can, the wider
and easier spheres of action. Unregenerated woman makes
a common cause with the serpentine head, and receives its
honors and rewards, but as the daughters of light are not
willing to do this, the conflict goes on.

Woman is claiming suffrage. It is a question in many
minds whether any form of representation as at present
existing amounts to much, or whether it is not after all only
a cleverly managed and ingeniously arranged sleight of hand
performance for the benefit of the wire pullers. Your Leg-
islatures do not represent one-eighth of the men who vote.
The United States Senate does not represent one-twentieth
of the men who vote. Can you wonder that the extraordinary machine you call government, from which one-half of
the average intelligence and fully one-third of the property
of the country is entirely excluded should be so very con-
summate a failure? It is known that some of the best and
ablest men in America have withdrawn themselves from
politics. If the suffrage is granted to woman under existing
conditions, the women who minister to the serpentine head
will continue to do so, and receive its honors and rewards;
but if the daughters of light come to the front, the daughters
of light, who can neither be bought, sold or terrified, then
a different and stranger thing will be made manifest; then

will be understood the saying of the Master: If new wine be poured into old bottles, then will the bottles burst and the wine be spilled. So when the woman element, which belongs to the new dispensation, and the new government, and can only come into its place when it is subjected to its laws, attempts to force its way into old conditions, the consequence will be that old conditions, or the old bottles of old governments will burst to pieces.

Then the last desperate effort to unite the scattered and falling serpentine power will be made under the man of sin, who will honor the God of forces, the distinctively masculine God, and despise the desire of woman for freedom and representation.

The German poet, Goethe, in his wonderful poem of Faust, has portrayed the unsatisfied longings and desires of the Transitional Period.

Faust has mastered all the sciences; he has arrived at the understanding of the natural forces and their application, and being hungry for the spiritual, and not knowing how to reach it divinely, has given himself over to Magic. This is a very distinctive feature of the Transitional Period; the consulting of spirits for earthly aims and to gratify earthly desires. Reinforcing selfishness, greed and sensuality, by the aid of the demoniac powers. Is any light attained in this manner? Not so, but rather darkness.

Look at the wonderful inventions of to-day; look at that most common fact, the cars. I never see the bright eye of the locomotive of the express train in the distance, and then hear its tremendous whirr and lightning rush but I repeat to myself the prophetic description of the strange object given by Isaiah more than two thousand years ago—"they shall seem like torches; they shall run like lightning."

Boundless Ophirs have been opened—Californias, Australias. They travel to and fro throughout the earth, and knowledge is increased. The English word "globe trotter" expresses quite a large class of these runners to and fro; but for all this, the spirit of the age is weary, so weary that suicide and insanity are constantly increasing—and in the poem Faust is about to drink the poison that shall end his exist-

ence. All at once he hears the sound of those sweet Easter
hymns that recall his childhood's old belief. He stays his
purpose, but the effect is only transitory. After a while the
tempter comes to him in a visible form, and whispers of the
joys of sense. He breathes into him the materialistic spirit,
which is as indifferent as nature is to the sufferings of the
beings whom her storms and tempests hurl to destruction.
He speaks of Margaret, plans their meetings under infernal
auspices, and draws the gentle girl into the fiery vortex. Borne
away in a torrent of delirious feeling, an unresisting victim
of the serpentine power, she sees but Faust—everywhere, his
form, the laughing glance of his eye, and *ach sein kuss*. He
drinks with her the charmed cup, and leaves her the poisonous dregs, the pangs, the torment; later, the prison and the
scaffold. Here is the whole of the transitional period in a
nutshell. It has abandoned the old landmarks and given
itself over to magic. The heart hungers for love, but the
woman who loves becomes the prey of man's selfishness.

Woman, too, makes selfish calculations on her power of
magnetic attraction, using it as a means of living, as a
means of success in the world, a mighty and cunning engine
of power over the hearts of others. Men and women insanely
trifle with each other, and lay profane and frivolous hands
on the divine ark. Every newspaper, the field of observa-
tion of every thoughtful man or woman, is filled with incidents that recall the strange power of the evil eye of the
Orientals. A dancing girl not long ago had the power to
send two men to a suicide's grave, and one of them ended
his existence over the grave of the other. A young Italian
girl was smitten by the same influence in this city, and she,
too, ended her days by poison in the presence of her un-
worthy lover. Alas for mortality, when the strongest of the
powers has us in its grasp, the force which must either be subjected to the divine and made the savor of life unto life, or
being seized upon by the powers of evil, is made the savor
of death unto death. The charm of the snake can only be
broken by a divine counter-charm, and this must be done
before woman can rise to her divinest position, and man and
woman enter a paradaisical condition. It is not God's anger,

but his love, that is going to be the destructive agent to all that is opposed to eternal law. Is it anger that makes the sword of the patriot a destroying force? No; it is the passion of his love for honor, truth and liberty. The fever excitement of the transitional period is one effect of the incoming tidal wave of divine love. Who shall dwell with everlasting burnings? He that hath clean hands and a pure heart.

Divine love is the cause of the tribulation of the last time, because it burns up, urges and drives to madness all but those who can walk through the furnace seven times heated because the Son of Man is by their side. Woman in the transitional period must pass through the furnace of passion changed by the presence of the Son of Man into the warmth and radiance of divine love. She walks there unharmed and smiling, because He is by her side, and there is not even the smell of fire upon her garments. The presence of the Lord in the light and glory of full sanctification is the only refuge of the sons and daughters of light in the day that is coming and is even now here. A strong rock is our God. The fire of divine love guards the access to the tree of life, watched over by the cherubim; hence the shortening of the days and the years of the life of those who go down into the chambers of death, the house of the strange woman; hence the ability to walk in the fire of those three who had faith and feared not, realizing the promise that "Where two or three are gathered in My name, there am I in the midst of them."

It is a peculiar feature of the present period that many men and women find themselves alone, separated. Families are being broken up as they never were before. Unsuitable relations between men and women are becoming intolerable to both parties. The most ancient Indian book says that woman is stronger than man; that she is an incarnate force, because man can subdue the elephant and the tiger and the natural world, but is himself tamed and subdued by woman. This is one side of a great truth. It is the revelation of the feminine force of the divine in woman that is agitating the world to-day as it was never agitated before. Man has always dreaded this, and it has been wisely held in check. The disciplines of thousands of years have been required to do for woman what the slavery of four hundred years had to teach the Hebrews. Woman is now about to receive a new, God-given law, while she passes through the transitional desert, ere she reaches the promised land. It will be no easy pilgrimage. Pilgrim sisters, fear not; look not back to the succulent meats of Egypt; cry not out for dainty meats; say not, at your peril, that your soul loathes the light bread of the wilderness, else, verily, ye shall die and not see the promised land.

The most ancient East is stirred. European Theosophists in Bombay are affiliating themselves with Asiatic rites and Indian magic.

How much more hopeful than this is the great native Hindoo movement of the Brahma Somaj, which, being interpreted, means Church of God. This, under God, is awakening the Hindoo heart, so long crushed under the domination of stronger, or rather, coarser peoples. It is remarrying widows, bringing Indian womanhood from the seclusion of the Zenanas to gladsome light and liberty. The Light of Asia, her awakened womanhood, now steps forth tenderly, gracefully, sweetly into the sunlight, and blends her oriental insight and loving devotion with the eagerness and fervor of her western sisters.

Mrs. Booth, one of the marked women of the period, is claiming the streets of London for the Lord, and in conjunction with her noble husband and children, is sending forth battalions of the sons and daughters of light all through the world. They are inviting to the supper, going into the highways and byways and compelling them to come in.

In the hill country of Bassim, India, a woman, often alone with her bands of orphans and young girls, calmly fronts the hoary immemorial religions and ancient temples and goes forth singing and preaching through the bazaars, bearing everywhere the banner of her Master. The profoundest minds of England are stirred with a love of India and the Indian people they have held by the sword so long. And it is time. Mohammedanism is gaining ground in India.

Village after village is being converted to that pitiless religion. The polygamous Mormon is in our midst to-day with all the craft, cunning and sensuality of the polygamous Mohammedan. The Mormons have known how to tame woman, subdue and utilize her, and Americans gaze upon the spectacle, some with disgust, others with considerable inward satisfaction. The toiling classes of England and Scandinavia, simple, eager, honest and impulsive, have furnished them with splendid material for their peculiar system. The Morrisites made the first break for liberty in the Territory, led by an inspired and remarkable man. The convincing Mormon arguments of cannon ball and rifle shot poured for three days into a camp of men, women and children, dispersed them and killed their leader. I do not know what were the opinions of the body of that people during their organization, and in the lifetime of their leader, upon the woman question.

I will now direct your attention to a very remarkable society, which lives, labors and flourishes at the present day. God does not work as man works. He puts down the mighty from their seat and exalts the humble and the meek. An obscure English woman, Ann Lee, appeared about the end of the eighteenth century. She· was the wife of a blacksmith and could neither read nor write, yet she was one of the Pivotal women of the Transitional Period. To her was unfolded the Fatherhood and Motherhood of God, a doctrine that had been but dimly apparent, and is not yet fully manifested. This doctrine man, with his intellectual strength and physical power, has almost overshadowed. It has become almost like the pale shadow of the moon around the crescent. This knowledge was placed in an earthen vessel that it might be manifest that the excellency of the power was of God and not of man. It was shown forth in humble and almost grotesque forms, that the worldly and light-minded might not interfere with it or disturb it.

Mother Ann, as she was affectionately styled, was herself the symbol of the idea that was given to her, though she did not know it. Ezekiel, the prophet, was made a symbol

unto his people, doing as the Lord commanded him, taking
a tile and portraying upon it the image of Jerusalem, taking
an iron pot and setting it for a wall between himself and the
city, which was portrayed on the tile, laying upon his side
and eating defiled bread, as the Lord commanded him.
All this must not only have seemed silly, but disgusting to
his people, but he obeyed. So did Ann Lee. She came to
America with her associates, and in faith and tribulation
founded the Order of Shakers. The name was attached to
them in derision, but many a true word has been spoken in
jest. It is the practical revelation of the divine motherhood in woman that to-day is the cause of the world's shak-
ing and agitation.

The associates set to work humbly and lovingly as they
were shown. They cultivated the ground, raised seeds and
plants, and were honest in their dealings. After a while
their various products acquired a commercial reputation.
But it was not time for the truth to be fully revealed, and
so the grotesque dresses, the peculiar dances, and various
other parts of their discipline, hid from the eyes of the
multitude its immense significance, and preserved the light
burning like the sacred light of Rome, tended by vestal
hands.

Ann Lee was a simple, truthful, earnest woman. There
have been others in this period brilliant, cultured and
inspired, like our own Margaret Fuller, and yet Brook
Farm, which assembled some of the most brilliant men and
women in America to experiment upon community life, was
a failure, and yet it was not a failure to the parties engaged
in it. It was probably a very rich experience. It left nothing permanent as to the individual material effort,—only a
radiance and a warmth in literature and in thought, that
may yet bear fruit,—but the simple obedience of a poor
English woman has produced permanent and visible results.
Noble Madame Rolands there have been, and brilliant
De Staels, but have they left behind them so much as Ann
Lee did with her one simple, noble title of mother? Mother
and father are the two noblest names that can appertain to
humanity, and ought to be the most consecrated. The

mother in Elizabeth of England, the mother in Josephine
of France is what preserves their names in lasting fragrance.
The distinctive Shaker tenet, as expressed in the Shaker
Roll, is that fleshly lust, fed by indulgence and gratifica-
tion, will never suffer souls to enjoy harmony and union
farther than the bonds of natural private families extend,
and even they come short. It was announced that the time
had come when a separation between flesh and spirit must
take place. It was also said that all associations that have
been formed for temperance in eating and drinking are the
operations of Divine Providence in the hearts of men to
prepare for mercy and judgment. This church was never
established as a popular show to the inhabitants of the
earth, to compass sea and land for proselytes, "but her people
were required to embody their strength in one united
capacity, to conquer and subdue their own evil natures
within, and gain a substance of the true oil and light of life
eternal. I have never promised salvation or protection to
any souls except in the path of my revealed will and order.
I will know no man by his words, but by his fruit. Then
the cogent question is asked: Have you found the golden
cord of purity which binds souls in one, or do the bands of
sin and death yet surround you and cause you to be broken
in pieces?"

In 1838, the manifestations of spirits in various Shaker
communities became frequent, and a vision of the war
of the rebellion was given. April 24, 1862, it was told
to a member of the order that fires, pestilences, earthquakes and famines should prevail, and towns should sink;
also, that droughts, earthquakes, wind and rain should destroy rich-loaded fields of vegetation. It was declared that
the Day of Judgment has commenced, and that the late
universal outpouring of God's Spirit among His chosen
people is here. It was declared that troubles still heavier
than those of the rebellion await the rulers and people of
this country. The seer said: "I was commanded to turn
my eyes to the north, and I saw the inhabitants walking to
and fro friendless, destitute and forlorn, gnawing their
tongues with anguish of soul, while their bodies were fam-

ishing with hunger. I looked to find the Israel of God, and beheld, as it were, wings gathering them together and hovering over them. I observed that all who gathered beneath these holy wings were safely protected, and in a low and pleasant vale, united as in one body. Your noble dwellings, where men have dwelt in ease and indolence, shall be places where food shall be prepared for the servants of God, and sweet industry shall reign. In many an unfinished shed, in barns and cottages of the poorest peasant, shall the power, mercy and justice of God be displayed, and His word loudly echo: To the meanest hovel shall some of the most renowned on earth yet gather, and on their bended knees seek the forgiveness of their God and humbly beg for his mercy, and by those whom they once disdained to comfort with the necessaries of life, shall they be fed with the imperishable bread of Heaven."

Such are some of the Shaker prophecies of events to occur in the Transitional Period. Some of them have been fulfilled; others are yet in the future.

This is a period of strange and eventful lives, of wonderful illuminations, of singular splendors, like our crimson sunsets with their glows and after glows of changeful colors.

The Communion of Saints, which we are privileged to enjoy, the outpouring of the Holy Ghost, which comes to those who open their hearts to invite it, the bliss and peace of sanctification, is our preparation for these trial times. These times of struggle and sorrow will bind women more strongly to each other; they will be more helpful to each other. The great temperance movement is energized by woman's efforts and her prayers, in private and in public works. Oh, what a divine blessing is being poured out on some of our churches; what a blessing is being poured forth outside of our churches. I tremble, yet rejoice exceedingly. It is the Pentecostal blessing before the tribulation. What is light and warmth to us is fire and destruction to the elements opposed to us. Our God is Love, but He is a consuming fire, and yet a place of light, warmth and blessedness. Hence, the anger and persecution a Pen-

tecostal period is apt to bring on the part of those opposed
to it.

Women are pressing forward in many departments of industry, showing the way in which we may work and provide
for the imminent future—in silk culture, horticulture, and
even agriculture.

Thrice blessed are they who are seeking to rekindle the
light of home in all the various departments of woman's
work. A true woman does not love the heartless crowding
of the factory. She is willing to work, if she can only have
a home, and homes are the price of industry.

The two great women writers of France and England, who,
strangely enough, in their published works appear under the
names of George Sand and George Eliot, were women of the
period, passionate, fervid and suffering. George Sand lived
her life and left us Consuelo, the sublime portrait of a woman
who overcame through love, who gave grace to poverty, and
joyfully accepted renunciation. George Eliot left us Romola,
a heroine of the cross, yoked together unequally with the
fickle, false and sensuous Tito, but triumphing through love
and patience even in apparent defeat. The difficulty is in
selecting the marked women of the transitional period, so rapidly and strongly is it calling forth the feminine in every
department—the heroines of anti-slavery, the heroines of
temperance, the valiant soldiers and officers of the Salvation
Army, the heroines of revolt against oppression throughout
the world.

The surging tide of the feminine is everywhere rising in
obedience to the attraction of the heavenly powers, as the
tides of the sea rise to the attraction of the moon.

Romola and Consuelo represent woman in the epoch of
transition, sustained by the divine ideal. Consuelo smooths
the road for her beloved Albert, who struggles with the
blindness of his age and its want of comprehension of the
divine truth that fills his soul. She stands by his side, and
their work and love is equal and happy. Romola walks
alone, sweet and silent, and tames her proud heart to fulfill
her lowly mission.

In a mild day of March, passing a warm, sunny nook, the

sense is smitten with a sudden fragrance, and looking down, a thicket of rich blue blossoms appears near an old tree stump; so comes the fragrance of the lives of some of the women of the transitional epoch, often very humble ones, violets hidden beneath the leaves, but they say that summer is coming.

Modern Spiritualism has called forth a majority of women into its ranks as its exponents. All classes and conditions of spirits have returned, eager to demonstrate their presence. It has been a living protest against the materialism of the eighteenth century, which almost denied the existence of spirit or of life beyond the tomb.

Many years ago a woman appeared in Dodworth's Hall, New York, for a short time. She was very beautiful—a pure Greek face and wealth of golden hair. She spoke ably, logically and most eloquently, before a large audience of some of the most cultured and thoughtful people of that city. After the lecture she answered many questions that were put to her, most satisfactorily to the questioners. Yet that woman had but a few weeks before graduated, not from college, but from the housemaid's broom and dust-pan. I have never heard of her since. Cora Richmond has been for forty years a channel of communication with the unseen world, and has faithfully and gracefully fulfilled her mission.

Some years ago a woman flashed like a meteor through the land. She had known the depths of poverty. She had known the insult and degradation of a neglected and forsaken wife. She inherited an intense and passionate temperament. She identified herself with modern Spiritualism and became its president; not only so, but she laid hands on Wall street, and she and her sister opened a stock broker's office there. She also published a paper which at that time attracted great attention. Then she stirred the people in the lecture field, and astonished even the reporters by her beauty and her boldness. Individuality and the power of the will of unsanctified woman never had a more fitting or splendid representative; but the rocket sent up its swift flame, and came down in splendid stars, and that was all; so much apparent achievement, so fine a light, and yet no line of radiance left after it—so it was with Victoria Wood-hull.

The media of the spirit would come with no direct message like the prophets of old. They are liable to be somewhat contradictory in their assertions. They are Eolian harps, played upon by breathings from the unseen. They speak of lives, conditions and surroundings, sometimes those of near and dear ones, in a land far off and yet so near. If the creatures that sing and fly could communicate with the finny inhabitants of the deep, it would be difficult to convey to the fishes the way in which birds exist. So we must wait for our own translation fully to realize it. We know that what makes our joy here will make our joy or sorrow there. There is a dual force in that world as in this. There are voices that come to us unsought, sweet, and calm, and fragrant with the gales of Heaven, but when driven by the winds of earthly desires, to seek wilder gales of spirit force to waft us to our desired haven, we risk loss and shipwreck. I will say, with sorrow, that some utterances I have heard from mediumistic persons remind me more of inspirations from angels who have lost their first estate from willfulness and disobedience than of anything divine. There is a proud boast of human will and of what is called individuality, such as Lucifer might have displayed. The unbridled human will is the fittest channel for demoniac possession.

Spiritualistic literature does not thrill me like the burdens of the Bible old. Emerson says:

> The litanies of nations came
> Like the volcano's tongue of flame
> Out from the burning core below,
> The canticles of love and woe.

A French writer says: "Thought and passion is the destructive social element. It is only by moderating the social activity of a people that we can insure its longevity." To-day all the forces are at work to stir up thought and passion in every class of society, even among those who have remained most solidly entrenched by ages of inertia, like the peasants of Russia. Devoted spirits, educated and wealthy men and women, and others are active in the revolutionary propaganda, even among this seemingly impenetrable class. It is the period of struggle from the old to the new, and we are all more or less feeling its unrest.

The various reforms in which the upheaving world spirit is trying to assert itself, give woman freedom.

Nihilism emancipated woman, and in return it owes much to the fervor and devotion of woman. All forms of labor agitation and social reform bring woman to the front, and so do the advanced inspirations of religious thought and religious work.

Men and women of the world held up surprised hands, because a band of Hallelujah Lasses were selling War Crys in the streets of Paris, and yet they could very complacently see bands of young girls trained to the service of the flesh nightly in every theatre in Paris.

Let woman come to the front for God and humanity. Who art thou that judgest another man's servant? To his own master he standeth or falleth!

CHAPTER IV.

THE NEW DISPENSATION.

There is a Restoration which is the theme of all prophetic song—a time of peace and harmony—when no galley with oars, or gallant war-ship shall pass up the place of broad rivers and streams, where the children of the kingdom dwell under the full manifestation of its glories. The wayfaring man that passes by, however simple he may be, cannot miss his way. There will be no tramps or vagabonds in the ordered kingdom of love. A period of very severe trial is said to precede this manifestation of the day of the Lord, and also the appearance of an Individual who is called the Man of Sin, who in his estate honors the god of forces, the power and strength of armies, and despises the desire of woman for freedom and representation, which desire holds the germ of the coming kingdom, which shall supersede his violence and brutality.

A few isolated lives of men and women have given us a foretaste of the sweetness and grandeur of these times. They have been like hot-house blooms in winter, but in the springtide of the New Dispensation, meadow and hillside shall be one carpet of blossoms.

Dr. James Hughes says: "The time is come when man on this planet is required by the eternal law of progression to receive new light and wisdom and new loves, through the agency of new conditions. Man has plucked almost all the fruits of the tree of knowledge, and partaken so freely of that which gratifies his egotism, that he is contemplating enthroning himself as God—the cause and end of all things."

There is a spiritual law to which all things, whether in heaven or on earth, must yield obedience. The changes and new conditions which are approaching are the effects of this divine law. Man to receive knowledge must slay innocence, therefore innocence is represented as a lamb slain from the foundation of the world. Experience is a progressive step to learn to know. In advancing in the dark, the feelings of innocence had to be suppressed, therefore was she slain; but innocence must revive again. The lion knowledge, and the lamb innocence, will lie down together and unite in harmony. This point is reached whenever man has truly learned himself, his relations to God and his fellow man and universal nature. Then will he from his dear-bought experience receive purity, which is sanctification, for knowledge will teach its necessity for individual happiness. Purity is innocence clothed upon with all the virtues, made manifest to the world in the practical life of Jesus of Nazareth. Changes in all human affairs are being rapidly effected under the controlling power delegated to Him. These changes commence with gigantic wars, and all who seek not the honor of God by manifesting peace on earth and good will to men, will be drawn within their terrible effects. When earthly governments are overthrown, anarchy will reign supreme. Then will God, through human agencies, bring order out of disorder, light out of darkness, and establish His government under Jesus, which will reach forth to all things in earth or heaven. Then will the Dragon, which is disorderly spiritualism, be chained, and the world thereby reduced to its right mind. Happy those who are prepared with the armor of God while this day of trial is passing through the world!

The just province or prerogative of government is, first, to educate the people in knowledge, both physical, intellectual, and spiritual. Secondly, to guard against all improprieties and infractions of these laws; and thirdly, to sustain, stimulate, and gratify the numerous faculties and noble aspirations of the soul or mind, thereby contributing to individual and universal happiness.

The first requisite in those who exercise government is wisdom and love, the next is power, and the third is system or order. The science of true government is perfect and sublime. The knowledge of the true principles on which a righteous government is to be established has not even reached man's comprehension in all its beauty and harmony.

For had it been understood, it would have manifested itself. It is man's most perfect attainment, and must therefore be victorious, and subdue all other governments. This condition not existing, it is evident that the science of government is not solved.

The true elements of government are contained within the constitution of man's own nature, slumbering until developed by the practice of his most noble energies, placing him in communion with the wisdom of the Highest. "The kingdom of God is within you." The divine mystery of government will be revealed and its power acknowledged in all the earth. For the wise and true must, by inherent law, subdue the unwise and untrue. Having emanated from the Highest, and being received into the most perfect faculties of man, it is loving, therefore powerful; it is wise, therefore just; it is true, therefore enduring.

The government of our Lord and Savior Jesus Christ is placed on an immovable basis, and will meet the aspirations of all the wise and good of mankind.

This power will destroy the soul of evil.

When man receives and assimilates the divine female aura of beauty and order, and when woman receives and assimilates the masculine inspiration of wisdom, then do they come into one equal and harmonious platform, and enter into a paradisiacal condition.

The crowning element of wisdom by which the feminine development is matured, is resident in and belonging to the male department of humanity. Woman eliminates a spiritual aura or pabulum for the sustenance of man's actions, energies, and perfections. She is more accessible to the angelic influences from whence is derived this pabulum or food of man. By partaking of this he is made capable of receiving a superior inspiration above that of woman, which is divine wisdom. Woman is accessible to this through man. Thus the circle is divinely formed. Woman is man's helpmate. She is the mother and source of man's most noble acts, as if she had directly performed them herself. In this way man's noblest thoughts and feelings have their origin in woman. Nature and God have constituted her to supply the pabulum for man's nourishment, both physically and mentally. Man receives his mental and physical growth from woman. He is the ripened fruit bearing seed, giving the finish to art, philosophy, government, and religion. Man's love is of a different nature from that of woman. It is alimentative, acquisitive, and appropriative. The true position of man and woman is ordained and unalterably fixed by God and Nature. The work of the new government will be perfectly finished by man under divine leadership, through and by woman's inspiring influence, proceeding quietly and powerfully from her formative soul. It is the man—child born of the woman—the world is thrilled with the hope of this birth.

The intuitive faculties of woman have felt and realized the fact of great wrongs existing in all governments. They realize a restlestness and apprehension of some strange revolution about to be inaugurated.

Liberty dawned in America and France, and lit within the heart of man a lively hope stimulating him to heroic acts and deeds of glory, establishing political freedom through most of this western continent. Next came the star of science distilling its fructifying influence, evolving new and astounding powers in machinery, and explorations of natural phenomena. The superior faculties have caught the glow sufficient to receive from the higher spheres a prophecy of something new and radical to be accomplished in governments.

Look at the insect world—see the unvarying perfection of the habitations of the bees, their cells and systematic government. Those perfect octagons are formed without line or compass. If we attribute this to their own intelligence, we must admit that it equals if it does not exceed that of the most accomplished human workman. These perfect cells are formed without experience or instruction, and never vary. It is instinctive automatic action—but man's intelligence is amplified with an individual sense of power and growth. His perfection is gradual.

Man's vast horizon is not spanned even by himself. He does not know his own possibilities. His intelligence has its source outside of particled matter, for all combinations of particled matter are decomposable, therefore mortal; but man's intelligence, from its power of control over matter in all its varied forms, and from its aspirations totally distinct from the automatic instincts of animal life, proves itself to be immortal.

Were it possible for man by any analytical means to ascertain the quality of life and motion, it would be found to consist of the most real substance within the regions of unbounded existence. From its virtue all things exist, in primitive, qualitative, relative order.

Love consolidates worlds. Intellect, unassisted by wisdom and the feminine power of love, cannot grasp the problem of a just and righteous government, or be prepared to realize it. Intellect does not always prepare the mind for the reception of wisdom. When intellect is wisely and divinely cultivated it bows before wisdom, and receives her as the cultivated field receives the rain.

Until man can realize the blending and co-operation of Wisdom, Knowledge, Power and Love in a harmonious union of its masculine and feminine expressions and earthly embodiments, the world will never be blessed with a true and righteous government.

When the masculine and feminine elements become subject to the guidance of Wisdom and Love under divine leadership, they will constitute the foundation elements on which to base a righteous government.

Under such an administration men and women would become new beings, manifesting the glory and beauty of their exalted nature, establishing peace, joy and happiness, and acknowledging the honor, dominion and power of those who in heavenly places have replaced the dominion of the evil powers who have held sway so long.

Uncomprehended faculties exist within us, which, when developed, will place us in happy contact with superior natures and superior wisdom. No one will be required to do more than they can accomplish with perfect satisfaction to mind and body. Reason, knowledge, wisdom and love will fraternize and preside over all the relations of life. A gov-

[53]

ernment to effect harmony and give universal satisfaction has, up to this time, not been possible. The same restless, ambitious character of mind that crept into one government and upset it, creeps into another. Whatever political party may arise from the turbid sea of present conditions will produce the same results, and therefore fail to meet human needs.

The aspirations and intuitive feelings, rightly directed, are the only base on which a permanent and righteous government can be predicated. These attributes require careful education and instruction from potent principles of power, love, wisdom and order—under whose teachings the wild, erratic ideas of power and dominion at present prevailing, will be reduced to a system of order, re-arranging and completely inverting their present mode of action.

Individualization will be changed into nationalization. Instead of government being as now, an institution organized for the protection of individual property, it will become the custodian of national possessions.

We have had power without wisdom. We have had wisdom and love manifested without power. The world has not yet been blessed by a leader exercising both power and love. Jesus was possessed of wisdom and love, but suffered the exercise of power to lie dormant. His most glorious victory was an apparent defeat; and his followers walk now by faith not by sight. In his coming kingdom he will manifest himself with power as well as love. Men will then understand how to exercise those leading qualities, the love of honor and the love of power. The places in that kingdom are prepared in accordance with eternal law, and are yielded neither to favoritism nor to earthly affection.

Woman can never take her place in old and fast-decaying existing institutions. She is a revolutionary force to destroy them. They cannot be mended. Years ago I had to say this to friends who were deeply interested in the suffrage movement. All my life, from my earliest recollection, I have had to say what seemed to me to be true, and it has almost always brought me in opposition to the ideas of those I most loved and valued. This has been a very great trial.

Woman is the soul of every revolutionary movement. She is impelled by a divine rage to right the wrongs of ages, not always wisely, for she does not see the whole of the programme, but with an unshrinking, fiery earnestness to do her part as she sees it in the present stress and direful necessity. Woman must appear more distinctively as mother, in all the grace and sweetness of that character.

For more than a thousand years Mother Mary has been held up before the eyes of the people. She has responded to the Infinite ideal, and represented the Divine Motherhood. The sorrowing human soul for centuries has sought refuge in her bosom. This idea, based upon an infinite truth, has been the strength of the Catholic Church. The stern reformers, the John Knoxes and the Calvins, who trampled upon Mariolatry, did not fully understand what they were doing. Mary was but a symbol of the Divine Motherhood. This has been held up before the people as some far-off, distant thing, but it is not so. It is near to us—even at our very door. This idea has to be taken from the traditions of the past, and revealed in the living present. We are the daughters of God, but it doth not yet appear what we shall be. We must not expect much help in man with his purely masculine traditions. Like Joseph, he will be often minded to put us away privily. Sanctified, redeemed woman can only come up to her position in the New Dispensation. Till then we walk by faith, not by sight.

The suffrage movement is a call from God, through woman, to revolutionize and re-arrange society and governments in all essentials. It is a cry that is being heard throughout the world. Its meaning is, "Prepare ye the way of the Lord, and make his paths straight."

The true order and position of man and woman is unalterably fixed by God and nature. Man can do nothing for his elevation or degradation without woman. Through her he is degraded to the chambers of death, or raised to life and light. It is her prerogative, power and nature to eliminate the spirit of all man's actions, as it is to eliminate their material bodies.

Her intuitions are swift, and often true, but her ambition, pride and selfishness has been the cause of unutterable woe to mankind; for this she owes humanity an incalculable debt.

He is neither a statesman nor an enlightened man who cannot appreciate and be touched by woman's call for liberty, truth, justice and temperance. Many suppose that this call arises from a desire for personal advancement, and to obtain liberty and security from oppression. It is true that this is the object of the agitation, and it will be accomplished, but in a different manner and through different means to what is expected. Let not woman destroy the serenity of her soul in present political conflicts. She does not belong to Cæsar, but to God.

The external in nature, containing the attributes of wisdom, strength, beauty and order, corresponds to the masculine. The sphere of the feminine corresponds with the internal or interior.

The beautiful, enviable powers and forces contained in magnetism, electricity, affinity, attraction, and many others, we will call feminine or internal. Man is the external, and like all external nature, he is the complement, or that which proceeds from the internal. Man is born of woman, as the grain is born of the earth.

If the mother side of the Elohim is not recognized by us to-day, it is not because it is not revealed in every pulse-beat and symbol, but from our incapacity to apprehend it. Man is the ultimate fruit containing the perfection of nature. Woman is the cause of all perfection in man, underlying by silent, potent forces, all manifestations of his beauty and deformity, his perfection and imperfection. Let her, as the mother of humanity, purify and cultivate love, tenderness, truth, charity, justice, inspiring hope and faith, and a determination to make manifest and develop the truths and principles relating to jutice, order and religion, that have not yet been manifested.

Raise thy head, oh, suffering Humanity, for the time will come when these principles will be understood and acted on in the kingdom of peace. Then will terror be driven

away, then will balm be poured into thy wounds, then will
end thy pain; beauty will be given for ashes, and life immortal for death. The victory over death will be made manifest in an orderly, divine manner. Even as Christ overcame so shall we.

Dear Humanity, live in hope; raise up thy tearful eyes.
Liberty, the fair daughter of wisdom, has baptized the
world with a few scintillations of divine glory not yet
understood, and known only by few. Many think that they
are of her counsels and fighting under her banner, but they
know her not.

Unprecedented prosperity and luxury have frenzied the
heart and brain of the rulers of this nation. They are adorn-
ing our groves and public places with the marble and bronze
statues of the founders of the republic. They are looking
on the Constitution they framed as capable of endurance
forever. We are exalting the instruments of support lent to
us in our weakness into gods to be worshiped. We are at
ease in our possessions, while the cries of the poor and mis-
guided are entering into the ears of the Lord God of
Sabbaoth. One rustling of the starry robes of Liberty is
sufficient to alarm the proud, whose eyes are dimmed by the
dust of gold, and who are blinded by the lust of official
power. There is no fixed point immovable, not even the
Constitution and Declaration of Independence. We are forever moving nearer to the fountain of love and wisdom, or
sinking away further from it. God was the teacher of our
fathers; from the same source we may derive yet higher
inspirations on laws and government.

Hear what Mazzini says: "Humanity is wandering in the
void, seeking the new bond destined to link together in religious harmony all the individual beliefs, presentiments and
activities now lost in the isolation of doubt. It invokes and
foresees the coming of a vaster unity destined to combine in
holy harmony the two terms tradition and conscience; a
unity which, starting from the foot of the cross, shall gather
together all the various religions in one sole people of
believers. All the political questions that occupy the
nations can only be set at rest by the solution of this prob-

lem." In another place he says: "*Seek in woman not merely a comfort, but a force, the redoubling of your intellectual and moral faculties."

Without his profoundly religious convictions, Mazzini could never have been sustained in his life of duty and sacrifice.

Without a profound idea of duty and simple faith and obedience, woman can never arrive at her sublime place in the New Dispensation. By discipline, by trial and sorrow, many are beginning to see and realize this, aspiring to become godlike instead of being dwarfed, and to reach the proportions of true womanhood as well as true manhood in Christ Jesus. Some of us fail sadly in reaching our ideal, but every mistake and error and failure keeps us learning more what we might be. Our ideas of what sanctification demands will enlarge and become more deep and profound as we realize its practical bearing in all the relations of life, particularly in the sanctity of the sexual relation. We are called to ascend into the kingdom of pure love and complete victory. Nothing is colder than sensuality; nothing is warmer than divine love. There is much to combat till children are rightly born. We bear a weight of ancestral traditions and misdirections. Woman has to leave much behind her when she turns her face towards Paradise.

The Hebrew prophecies are full of grand and cheering visions of the New Dispensation; sad and mournful burdens of sorrow for failure and weakness, alternate with joyful anthems and victorious pæans of final victory.

. In the latter part of the prophecy of Ezekiel he records his vision of a magnificent house, which appears to have been connected with a temple, and yet separated from it. This house was spacious, conveniently constructed, of noble proportions, with halls, courts, and galleries; and what appears to have impressed the mind of the seer, was that the triumphal palm was the ornament and distinguishing feature of the decoration of its glorious chambers and stately porticos; palm trees everywhere, on windows, arch, and gate, and even on the posts of the doors. It was orderly and beautiful; on the south were the dwellings of the priests having charge of the house, and on the north the dwellings of the priests having charge of the altar. But in all this the seer saw no sign of present human habitation, for it was the vision of things yet to be.

After he had seen the house, he was shown the temple, with its stairs ever winding upward in spiral progression, emblematic of the connection of the earth with the interior heavens.

There was a striking difference between this temple and the house destined for human habitation though not yet inhabited; for the palm trees here alternated with the images of the cherubim, showing that this temple and inmost sanctuary was inhabited by angelic beings, while the house, which was apparently destined for human habitation, was not yet inhabited. This inner temple had folding doors, destined to be thrown open to the widest possible extent. It had also galleries, and fair prospects, north, south, east, and west. But except the angel who measured and surveyed the temple, no human form was seen.

Then the prophet was brought to the gate of the temple that looked eastward, and the appearance of the vision that he had seen by the river Chebar passed before him, the many-eyed cherubim, the wheels instinct with life and fiery flame, emblematic of the eternal deific forces of life and motion, and the glory of the Lord filled the temple, and the earth shined with his glory; and it was said " this is the law of the house upon the top of the mountain, the whole limit round about shall be most holy;" corresponding with what another prophet says—"that the Lord's house shall be established on the top of the mountains, and all nations shall flow unto it."

The prophet was told that this consecrated eastern gate should be open on the Sabbath day and day of the new moon, but be closed the six working days. Afterwards he was brought again to this eastern gate, and saw waters issuing from under the threshold eastward, and these waters increased rapidly in volume—from a stream that would only wet the ankle to one above the knees, and then it became a mighty river that could not be passed over.

The angel then brought him to the brink of this mighty river, which the seer John saw long after in the isle of Patmos, and Ezekiel saw as John did, trees on either side of the river—very many trees on one side and on the other—trees whose leaf shall not fade, neither shall their fruit perish; and it was said that the reason why these trees were fadeless was because they were fed by the water of life which issued out of the sanctuary where the heavenly splendors had shone. The Shekinah had filled the temple with life and opened the source of the waters of life to gladden the earth.

This vision has a far wider signification and scope than Ezekiel probably realized. Many of the children of the west have called the Jewish creed narrow; but, like a strong ark made for stormy seas, it has floated where many a proud argosy has gone down.

The Americas at this time were veiled in darkness—the dominant Anglo-Saxon race had yet to be born. Australias and New Hollands were as unknown as the geography of Jupiter.

To no glory of the second temple reared upon the ruins of the first is this splendid vision applicable.

Rising from the ruins of the present social order, that vision will appear in all its august beauty.

It designates the great social, governmental and religious reconstruction of the future, an order of life that shall combine in a remarkable manner, social and material well being, with spiritual advancement. No human form was seen in the great house, so triumphantly decorated with its capitals of palm. It was the vision of the times of the restoration of all things of which God has spoken by the mouth of His holy prophets since the world began. It was also blended with a prophetic view of the restoration of Israel, of the borders of the twelve tribes, and the allotted portion for the Prince, the Shiloh that is to come.

Nearly the whole of the planet, with the exception of the Polar regions, is now unveiled. The hitherto almost unknown half of the social sphere, which is divine womanhood, is becoming unveiled.

The hidden west, the woman side of life, with all its un-reached capabilities, has yet to be made manifest ere the scope of this wonderful vision can be clearly understood. A dubious twilight may precede that bright day, but it will rise at last.

The dominant note of all I have had to say is the true position of woman in God, or rather the shining forth of God through woman.

Fully sanctified, she enters into a safe place and can re-trace her steps back to lost Paradise, her Heavenly inherit-ance, where she can stand side by side with man without subjection and without fear.

I have always felt that Christ was, in a special sense, the friend of woman. When she had no other friend on earth, when she was even a sinner and an outcast, he protected and blessed her. It is even so to-day. He is an eternal refuge.

The woman question is a question of development, not of self-assertion.

Woman is what she is, and she is developing more and more into the ideal of divine womanhood as the divine womanhood is manifested through her. When that is fully manifested, she will come into her place naturally, with a divine power and grace.

Until then the coming Kingdom cannot be manifested—the brotherhood cannot be fully manifested without the divine harmony of the sexes.

When that is accomplished, woman will cease to be revo-lutionary, because there will be no need of the revolutionary element, but the revolutionary element will more and more disturb nations and families until this is accomplished.

From the mother's womb, from her bosom are the ele-ments of the future world created, and when motherhood becomes divine, instead of as it sometimes happens less than human, the angels will rejoice.

Then the full orbed sphere of humanity, equally balanced in both its hemispheres of opposite sexes, will sail harmoni-ously through the heavenly blue. The wail that comes from our wretched planet and disturbs the elemental harmony will cease, and she will sing with the morning stars, and all the sons and daughters of God will chant the new bridal song.

It may be said that Christ did not fully declare this while on earth. He said: "I have many things to say unto you, but ye cannot bear them yet." Perhaps some things were left for the bride to declare.

I feel more and more persuaded that the germ of the New Dispensation is a humble people,—known, as violets are known, by their hidden fragrance. These will all know the Lord from the least even unto the greatest.

This is the real substance of all former ceremonies and church rituals, of whatever nature, even as the Gospel fulfilled the Jewish law and made it honorable while it replaced it. It is a natural outgrowth, without conflict and without schism. The true Ecclesia,—the church or assembly of the faithful. Without woman as mother, this cannot be. Now as never before she is wakening to her duties, her responsibilities, and her privileges.

SAN FRANCISCO, November, 1884.

www.ingramcontent.com/pod-product-compliance
Lightning Source LLC
Chambersburg PA
CBHW022155020726
47496CB00008B/2730